Skills I Wish I Learned in School

Building a Research Paper

Everything You Need to Know To Research and Write your Paper

Nicole Lusiani

dirtpath
PUBLISHING

Alameda, California

First printing February 2012

Published by
Dirt Path Publishing
P.O. Box 2623
Alameda, CA 94501

To order
Dirt Path Publishing Order Department
P.O. Box 2623
Alameda, CA 94501
Tel: (510) 239.7157
Online: DirtPathPublishing.com
Email: Info@DirtPathPublishing.com

**Bulk pricing is available for educators and educational organizations.
Please include this request with your inquiry.**

Forthcoming Books in the Series

Skills I Wish I Learned in School

Managing My Money

Navigating My Personal and Professional Relationships

For my students, past and present,
who make this crazy job absolutely worth the effort.

Welcome!

You have purchased this handbook because you are in need of some guidance in the research paper process. What makes this "how-to" different is that it is clear and concise, with step-by-step processes that detail what to do, how to do it, and in what order. I've also taught this process to over one thousand students. You need help? I'm the one to teach you.

Anytime you want to find information about something, you are conducting a form of research. Let's say you are looking for something to do; an Internet search for "activities" is going to get you thousands of options and almost all of them will be irrelevant. What do you most want to do? Eat? What do you want to eat? How far are you willing to travel? How do you know the restaurant you chose any good? Go to the restaurant's site and they say they're great, but are they *really*? Your restaurant search and analysis is strikingly similar to the academic research process. This handbook will show you how to choose, focus, and organize your research so you can write a strong paper.

We call this "building" a research paper because that's exactly what you'll be doing: putting it together step by step. There are many styles of academic research; the one provided in this handbook is designed to give you a foundation for your skills. Once you are an expert researcher you will be able to stretch and find your own style. For now, let's focus on the basics.

The skills in this handbook can work for any curricular discipline because the skills of research and persuasive writing come up in all content areas. However, there are some ideas that might not match up exactly. For example, where I use the word "thesis," others might use the word "claim," where I use the word "claim" others might use the word "argument," and so on. Be careful not to get hung up on the particular vocabulary and focus, instead, on building your research skills. As I said before, this book gives you the basics; I trust you will continue to build toward your specific needs and interests as you move forward.

One more point: topic choice is critical. When conducting academic research you may struggle at times with the required steps. The only way to make this bearable is to have an interesting topic about which you want to know more. Take your time with all the steps provided in this handbook, most especially topic choice.

Thank you for choosing this handbook as your guide toward building a research paper. Have confidence in your ability to make it happen. You have everything you need to build toward your own success.

Sincerely,

Nicole

Table of Contents

<u>Finding My Topic</u>

This is the most important decision of the entire process. You will spend a lot of time with this topic; as such, it needs to be something that interests you.

- Consider the parameters and/or requirements provided by your instructor. Within them, consider the best and most interesting possible topic options for you.

- Once you have some topics under consideration, think about what makes you curious. Curiosity is a great motivator so explore what you want to know, what questions you have, what you'd ask if you could. Once those potential topics are listed on paper, proceed.

- Make a list of your top options. Bring the list to your instructor for feedback.

- If you still have multiple options on your list, do a quick search on the Internet. There should be enough information for you to research, but not so much that you will end up repeating what has already been said. This paper is NOT a book report, it's a research paper; that's an important difference. This will be clarified further at a later point.

- Using the Internet, your textbook, family, and friends, conduct a background check on your topic and/or questions. What do they know about it? When did it happen? How did it affect people? See Appendix A if you need a list of suggested questions.

- The purpose of this background check is two-fold: one, you want to make sure you are going to enjoy researching this topic, and two, you are gathering information you may end up using in your introduction and/or conclusion.

See Appendix A for a sample background check handout.

Where Do I Start

Compiling research and writing a paper can begin one of two ways. Read through each option and then decide which you want to pursue.

Option 1: Backward Mapping	Option 2: Frontward Mapping
Backward Mapping means starting with the end goal and planning backward. Choose this option if you want to prove a particular point and/or already have a clear destination for your paper.	**Frontward Mapping** means starting with step one and moving forward. Choose this option if you are clear about your general topic but you are open as to the point you want to prove and/or your end destination.

Option 1: Backward Mapping

1. **Establish Your Thesis.** Develop the point you will prove with your research.

2. **Breakdown Claims.** Break the thesis down into more manageable parts.

3. **Find Sources.** Find trustworthy sources.

4. **Note Evidence.** Collect accurate facts that support your position.

5. **Pause.** Find your research gaps and figure out how you need to proceed.

6. **Revise.** Decide if your research fits your overall thesis and your claims.

7. **Collect Further Evidence.** Keep at it!

8. **Final Outline.** Order your evidence in a way that best tells the story.

9. **Draft.** Write, edit, revise, edit, complete.

Specific directions begin on page 4.

Option 2: Frontward Mapping

1. **Breakdown Ideas.** Identify parts that, together, will be your overall topic.

2. **Find Sources.** Find trustworthy sources.

3. **Note Evidence.** Collect accurate facts that support your topic.

4. **Develop Thesis.** Develop the point you will prove with your research.

5. **Breakdown Claims.** Break the thesis down into more manageable parts.

6. **Collect Further Evidence.** Keep at it!

7. **Pause.** Find your research gaps and figure out how you need to proceed.

8. **Collect Further Evidence.** Keep at it!

9. **Pause.** Be sure thesis and claims are working, identify any remaining needs.

10. **Collect Last Evidence.** Almost done!

11. **Final Outline.** Order your evidence in a way that best tells the story.

12. **Drafts.** Write, edit, revise, edit, complete.

Specific directions begin on page 19.

Research Option 1: Backward Mapping

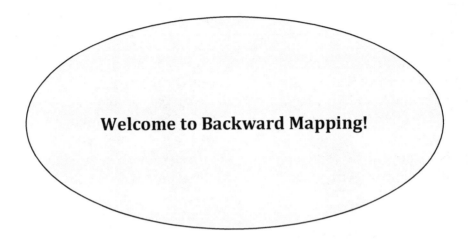

If you have chosen this option, you have a clear position on an interesting topic and are ready to begin. The following steps provide direction and examples for each part of the process.

All steps use the example topic, "Dropping the Atom Bomb to end WWII." This will give you a sense of how your topic should come together. See the Appendix for handouts that may be helpful to you as you complete each step.

Take a deep breath and trust yourself; if you were smart enough to get help from this handbook, you are going to rock this research!

Step One of Backward Mapping: Establish a Thesis

Remember we talked about this being a research paper and not a book report? A report is just a recounting of the facts; *a research paper uses facts written in a way that proves your thesis, or your position, on your topic.*

A thesis is not an announcement of your topic ("This paper will be about..."); it is your position on a topic. As such, your thesis should be strong, clear, concise, and without a doubt show the reader your position on the topic and the point you will prove with your research.

Sample Topic: Dropping the Atom Bomb to end WWII

This is a topic that is very interesting to me. I'm going to be spending quite a bit of time with this topic, so I chose something that made me not only curious, but motivated to research. (Never underestimate the power of an interesting topic!) For the sake of consistency, this sample will be used throughout this handbook.

Thesis Examples:

Below Average	Average	Above Average
• I think the U.S. was right to drop the bomb and you will too after reading my paper.	• The U.S. was right to drop the Atom Bomb on the Japanese in August of 1945.	• The United States was desperate to end WWII and since the Japanese had no intention of surrendering, the U.S. was totally justified in dropping the Atom Bomb.

Excellent
After four years and thousands of lives lost, by August 1945 the U.S. was desperate to end WWII. The government compiled strong evidence that showed the only way to bring the war with Japan to an end was to do something drastic and devastating; therefore, the U.S. was justified in dropping the Atom Bomb.

For each thesis example, notes about positives and negatives are as follows:

Below Average: I think the U.S. was right to drop the bomb and you will, too, after reading my paper.

- Is it grammatically accurate with correct spelling? Yes. That's the only thing keeping this thesis from the "poor" level.
- NEVER use "I think" in your thesis. It's clear you think that or you wouldn't be writing it. In addition, it invites the reader to say, "Well that's what you think, not what I think."
- NEVER use "you" anywhere in a research paper. You should be arguing a point, not talking to the reader. Stay focused and don't personalize it.
- There is no sense of context in this example. It might have happened yesterday in Nebraska for all we know.

Average: The U.S. was right to drop the Atom Bomb on the Japanese in August of 1945.

- The lack of "I think" and "you" automatically make this better.
- Context is present, but not specific.
- It's concise and clear, but short on depth.

Above Average: The United States was desperate to end WWII and since the Japanese had no intention of surrendering, the U.S. was totally justified in using the Atom Bomb.

- With concise, clear, and strong language, this is a solid thesis.
- There are, however, two overarching generalizations here: "no intention" and "totally justified." Change the language to that of research instead of judgment.

Excellent: After four years and thousands of lives lost, by August 1945 the U.S. was desperate to end WWII. The government compiled strong evidence that showed the only way to bring the war with Japan to an end was to do something drastic and devastating; therefore, the U.S. was justified in dropping the Atom Bomb.

- A two-sentence thesis is not always recommended or allowed in high school research papers. In college, sometimes a 3-5 sentence thesis is expected. Carefully review the guidelines provided by your instructor.

- Regardless of length requirement, be sure you note about our thesis above that it provides context, sophistication, and a strong sense that you know what you are talking about. For longer theses, consider adding a counter-clause, specific examples of what evidence you're going to include, and/or a "So what?" statement. (More information about these additions is available in the thesis checklist in the appendix.)

- There is a strong tone of educated research in this thesis. There is no judgment, no exclamation, just a calm sense of what was happening and what had to happen as a result.

- The reader is left with a strong sense of what your research will prove and trusts you to get on with doing it.

See Appendix B for a thesis checklist.

NOTE! Sometimes starting with the thesis is overwhelming. You know the general areas you want to cover and even what you want to say about them, but you don't feel quite ready to establish a thesis. Is this you? Consider moving on to the next section about claims first then, once your claims are done, you can come back here to build a thesis around those claims. This is very common, so feel free to test it out to see if it feels better.

Step Two of Backward Mapping: Breakdown Claims

Claims come directly out of your thesis.

To develop your claims, first break down your excellent thesis; second, make claims out of your pieces in a way that they both take a position and, when added up, prove your thesis. Follow the model below for direction.

Here's our excellent thesis:

> After four years and thousands of lives lost, by August 1945 the U.S. was desperate to end WWII. The government compiled strong evidence that showed the only way to bring the war with Japan to an end was to do something drastic and devastating; therefore, the U.S. was justified in dropping the Atom Bomb.

Here's our excellent thesis broken down into parts:

> 1-After four years and thousands of lives lost, by August 1945 the U.S. was desperate to end WWII.
>
> 2-The government compiled strong evidence that showed the only way to bring the war with Japan to an end was to do something drastic and devastating;
>
> 3-therefore, the U.S. was justified in dropping the Atom Bomb.

How Do I Make Claims out of these Parts?

Claims are like subtopics because they break down the thesis down into more manageable parts; but they are different because *claims take a position.* You will prove each claim one at a time through your research and, together, they will add up to prove your thesis.

Claim Examples

The following claims are ones that would strongly support the example thesis. Notice:

- Average claims are clear and concise, take a position, and clearly define the coming paragraph(s).
- Above average claims do all of the above, plus provide a bit of context.
- Excellent claims do all of the above with sophisticated, research-based tone and language. They also convey the same idea as part of the thesis with a bit more detail (and without using the same words).

Claim One Examples **based on "After four years and thousands of lives lost, by August 1945 the U.S. was desperate to end WWII."**

- **Average**: The U.S. was desperate.
- **Above Average**: After four years of bloody battle, the U.S. was desperate to end WWII.
- **Excellent:** Because the human and monetary costs of the war were spiraling and Americans at home were anxious both financially and emotionally, the U.S. government was desperate to end WWII.

Claim Two Examples **based on "The government compiled strong evidence showed that the only way to end the war with Japan was to do something drastic and devastating…"**

- **Average**: The government had evidence that the Japanese were not going to ever give up.
- **Above Average**: The U.S. government had strong evidence that drastic measures were required to end WWII.
- **Excellent:** Even as it appeared inevitable that Japan would eventually lose the war, it was clear that a drastic and devastating move by the Allies was necessary to force the surrender of the Japanese.

__Claim Three Examples__ based on *"...therefore, the U.S. was justified in dropping the* **Atom Bomb."**

- **Average**: The U.S. was justified in dropping the Atom Bombs.
- **Above Average**: Although there were other options to end the war, the U.S. was justified in dropping the two Atom Bombs on Japan.
- **Excellent:** President Truman was presented with other options to force Japanese surrender, however none of them would be as devastating as the dropping of the Atom Bombs on Hiroshima and Nagasaki, Japan.

See Appendix B for a claims checklist.

Step Three of Backward Mapping: Find Sources

Once your position is clear and is broken into manageable claims, you must find several pieces of accurate evidence for support. Below are basic guidelines to help you find the sources that are right for you.

Books/Periodicals

- Your instructor may want you to reference something called "scholarly articles." Your campus library should have an electronic catalog of articles on all kinds of topics. Read through the abstracts to find some that may be right for you.

- Check the publication/copyright year. You want a source that is fairly recent and/or with a recent update. The exception here is a highly regarded historical source that may be more timeless in its research.

- If you find a source you like, use its bibliography to find other books on the topic. If this author found them useful, you might too.

- Don't be put off by an old/big/boring-looking source. Read the table of contents and the index to see if has a topic you might be considering. Read the abstract and/or a page or two to see how it feels.
  It might surprise you.

Internet Sources

- Generally speaking, sites that end in .org and .gov are reputable because they represent an organization or they are government-based sites. However, there are many high quality .com sites as well; continue down this list to differentiate the valid from the less valid.

- If the site is sloppy, unorganized, and/or haphazard it almost always indicates you need to move to a different source.

- Avoid any website that exists to tear down another group or idea. This is a sure sign of slanted/one-sided views that are not based in quality research.

- Look for judgmental language vs. research based language ("This was a preposterous waste of time by the Americans…" vs. "This idea challenged many in the nation who believed…"). If judgment is infused in the language, it's most definitely slanted in research. Move on.

- If the site lists its sources, it's usually worth using. Anyone who takes the time to do so takes research seriously.

Find a Source You Like?

When you find a source worthy of using YOU MUST write down its publication information. Use Appendix C or just keep a list on binder paper. Whatever you do you must **WRITE DOWN THE FOLLOWING SOURCE INFORMATION:**

Book Sources

Title, author, publisher, city of publication, copyright

> ***Example****: War, by Thomas Jackson, Chronicle Books, NY, 1999*

Internet Sources

Author (if provided), title of the page you are using on this site, title of overall website, date of article/last date site was updated, date you viewed the site, website address

> ***Example****: Giovanni Antonio, "Allies," "WWII in America," June 2002, viewed November 8, 2010, www.ww2americans.com*

Periodical Sources

Author(s), title, volume, issue, year of publication, page numbers, medium of publication

> ***Example*** *Thomas Jackson, "Necessity of Nuclear Weapons," Military Quarterly, 25.2, 1996, print*

See Appendix C for a reproducible source list.

Step Four of Backward Mapping: Note Evidence

First you must know what evidence is:

1. It is something you did not know before you read it,

2. It is related to your general thesis and/or supports a specific claim.

Next, you must know how to document that evidence:

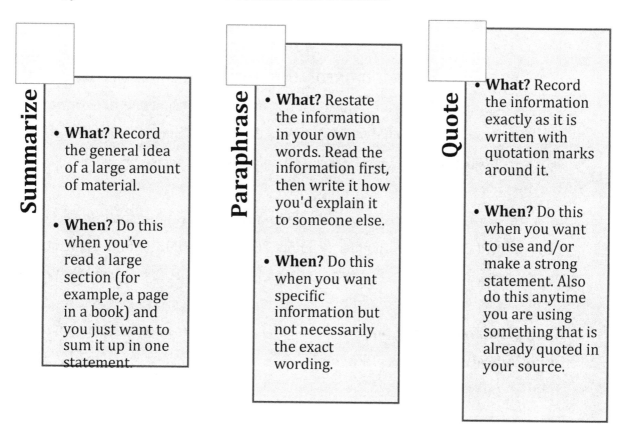

Summarize

- **What?** Record the general idea of a large amount of material.

- **When?** Do this when you've read a large section (for example, a page in a book) and you just want to sum it up in one statement.

Paraphrase

- **What?** Restate the information in your own words. Read the information first, then write it how you'd explain it to someone else.

- **When?** Do this when you want specific information but not necessarily the exact wording.

Quote

- **What?** Record the information exactly as it is written with quotation marks around it.

- **When?** Do this when you want to use and/or make a strong statement. Also do this anytime you are using something that is already quoted in your source.

There are many ways to take notes. By the time you have become an experienced researcher, you will have tried many ways to find the best fit for you. For now, however, you will use the note-card method. This will allow you to order the evidence you find in a way that best proves your position and tells the story of your research.

Follow the note-card method as directed on the following page, even if you don't see the point. If you TRUST THE PROCESS, the process will serve you. If you don't, you'll end up creating a lot more work for yourself in the long run.

Note-card process:

1. Once you deem a source reliable and useful, note its source information (see page 12) either on the provided source list (see appendix C) or separate paper. LABEL THE SOURCE with a letter (A, B, C, etc.).

2. All notes should be written on one side of a note card. Ideally these note cards are index cards (or even half-index cards), all of the same size.

3. PUT ONLY ONE PIECE OF INFORMATION ON EACH CARD. USE ONLY ONE SIDE OF EACH CARD. If your information goes on longer than one side of one card, you have too much. Even if it's a quote, break it in half using ellipsis (...) if you need to. It's best to keep your note to one phrase or sentence if possible.

4. Instead of writing the source's full publication information on this card, write the SOURCE LETTER. You must also note THE PAGE NUMBER for a book or periodical or the DATE VIEWED for an Internet source (see examples below).

A *sample note-card* for a <u>book</u> or <u>periodical</u> source looks like this:

A *sample note-card* for an <u>internet</u> source looks like this:

"The tactics of the Japanese indicate they will never surrender." President Truman, July 1945.

Source C, page 52

"The tactics of the Japanese indicate they will never surrender." President Truman, July 1945.

Source C, 3/25*

*This is the date you viewed the site

You may be tempted to number your cards as you write them; ***don't***. There will be a process for that later. For now, just stack the cards as you go, keeping them secure in an envelope, with a rubber band, or in an index cardholder.

Need a Guideline?

Find out from your instructor how many pages are required for your paper. Then gather about 6-8 cards for each page required (5 page requirement = about 30 cards). This will be a great start from which to launch step five.

See Appendix D for reproducible note cards.

Step Five of Backward Mapping: Pause

You now need to be certain your thesis and claims are working with your evidence so you can have specific direction for your last bit of research. "Pause" has three goals: **Organize** your information to see what you have so far; **Consider** the story you are trying to tell; **Proceed** with researching the evidence you still need to find.

Organize

1. Spread your cards out over a large surface so you can see and read all the evidence you have so far.

2. Make a pile of evidence for each of your claims. If you find your claims aren't clearly represented by the evidence you have, group them together logically and you can readjust your claims later by referencing back to pages 8-10. If you find a few of your cards don't quite fit, put them aside for now.

3. Within each claim pile, put the cards in an order that start to tell the story you aim to tell. You'll notice some gaps; that's the point of this whole activity. **This is a time to make what I call a "Remember!" sheet. This is where you'll keep track of all the things you want to remember as you proceed**. Make a note about your information gaps and move on.

4. Now that your claim piles are in order, decide which claim pile goes first, second, and so on.

Consider

1. Is your original thesis supported by your claims? If yes, proceed. If it's questionable, refer back to pages 5-7 to revise your thesis.

2. Are your original claims supported by the evidence you have found? It so, proceed. If it's questionable, refer to pages 8-10 to revise your claims.

3. After you've completed the two suggestions above, I'd strongly consider finding a friend or two to help you be sure you've considered all possibilities. Often times we know what we want to say and take for granted that we're saying it. Reading your information aloud to someone else is the best way for you to check your self and your work.

Proceed

1. Spread out the cards for your first claim pile again.

2. Reread your first claim and then reread the evidence you already have.

3. What more do you need to prove this claim? Is there a supporting statistic, a quote, a piece of information that would really prove your point to the reader? Go to your "Remember!" sheet and note what you need to find for claim one.

4. Restack your first claim pile and move on to the second claim pile. Repeat steps #1-3 for each of your claim piles.

5. Restack all claim piles into the one large stack. Add any loose cards to either the front or the back. Rubber band or clip your cards to keep them in this general order, but DO NOT number them.

Step Six of Backward Mapping: Collect Last Evidence

Now it's time to finish that research. Fill in your holes and get as much accurate, interesting evidence as possible to prove your claims and thesis.

Reminders:

1. Use high-quality sources. You may want to re-read page 11 to remind yourself what kind of sources are viable and which you should avoid.

2. If you are looking for something very specific, narrow your search accordingly. You no longer want to search online for "atom bomb" when you really want to know about what people thought about the bomb when testing it in New Mexico. In that case you'd search something like, "eyewitness accounts of atom bomb testing in New Mexico 1945."

3. If necessary, revisit pages 13-15 about rules for note-cards. Now is *not* the time to get lazy. Include every source on your source page and note every piece of evidence properly. Doing so now will save you a lot of time and grief in the long run.

4. You'll know you're done when you have plenty of strong evidence for each claim—both in quality and quantity. Until you do, keep researching.

When you are done with this process, proceed to the section on final outlines, drafts, and citations on page 38.

Research Option 2: Frontward Mapping

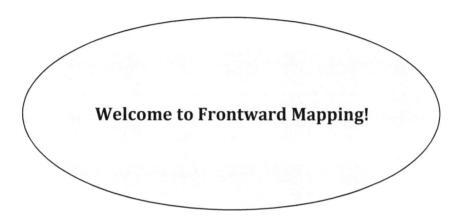

Welcome to Frontward Mapping!

If you have chosen this option, you have an interesting topic, but not yet a clear position. The steps below provide direction and examples for each part of the process.

The following steps use the example topic, "Dropping the Atom Bomb to end WWII." This will give you a sense of how your topic should come together. See the Appendix for handouts that may be helpful to you as you complete each step.

Take a deep breath and trust yourself; I know you can do it; you just need to remember that too.

Step One of Frontward Mapping: Breakdown Ideas

Your topic is likely still fairly broad; before moving on you should narrow your focus. This will help you now as you start to research and later when you develop your position. Do this in three steps: Brainstorm, Narrow and Expand, and Choose.

Here's what you do:

Brainstorm

1. CHOOSE SOMETHING THAT INTERESTS YOU!
   Your instructor will likely give you some guidelines, but within those brainstorm all possible options that peak your curiosity and interest. This is the best motivator to staying focused as you move through the process.

2. Say you are interested in WWII. This is an enormous topic. Get down on paper all the things you know about your topic, everything, in either list or a more visual web-like form. When you feel you've completely exhausted all possible options, move on.

   Example: 1939-1945, Pacific Theater, European Theater, home front mobilization, the role of women, segregation, code talkers, weapons, Pearl Harbor...

Narrow & Expand

1. First, choose your top 3-5 areas of interest from your brainstorm. Note them on the back of your brainstorm sheet.

2. It may seem odd to widen the topic further, but it is here you might find some nugget of great interest to you. For each of your top areas of interest, note everything you know about each.

Example: *Weapons—aircraft, weapons, land systems, ships and sups, large weapons/missiles, atom bomb*

Choose

Pick the part of this topic that is the most exciting and/or interesting to you. If you have changed course and/or narrowed significantly from when you originally chose your topic, conduct another "Background Search." Refer to Appendix A for more information.

This additional background search may seem like an unnecessary or redundant step. Move beyond that initial feeling and do it anyway. You will likely use this information in your introductory paragraph anyway, and it will give you a strong starting point from which to launch your research.

Step Two of Frontward Mapping: Find Sources

Once your topic is clear, you must find several pieces of accurate evidence

for support. Below are basic guidelines to help you find valid sources.

Books/Periodicals

• Your instructor may want you to reference something called "scholarly articles." Your campus library should have an electronic catalog of articles on all kinds of topics. Read through the abstracts of several to find ones that may be right for you.

• Check the publication/copyright year. You want a source that is fairly recent and/or with a recent update. The exception here is a highly regarded historical source that may be more timeless in its research.

• If you find a source you like, use its bibliography to find other books on the topic. If this author found them useful, you might too.

• Don't be put off by an old/big/boring-looking source. Read the table of contents and the index to see if has a topic you might be considering. Read the abstract and/or a page or two to see how it feels. It might surprise you.

Internet Sources

• Generally speaking, sites that end in .org and .gov are reputable because they represent an organization or they are government-based sites. However, there are many high quality .com sites as well; continue down this list to differentiate the valid from the less valid.

• If the site is sloppy, unorganized, and/ or haphazard it almost always indicates you need to move to a different source.

• Avoid any website that exists to tear down another group or idea. This is a sure sign of slanted/one-sided views that are not based in quality research.

• Look for judgmental language vs. research based language ("This was a preposterous waste of time by the Americans..." vs. "This idea challenged many in the nation who believed..."). If judgment is infused in the language, it's most definitely slanted in research. Move on.

• If the site lists its sources, it's usually worth using. Anyone who takes the time to do so takes research seriously.

Find a Source You Like?

When you find a source worthy of using YOU MUST write down its publication information. Use Appendix C or just keep a list on binder paper. Whatever you do, you must **WRITE DOWN THE FOLLOWING SOURCE INFORMATION:**

Book Sources

Title, author, publisher, city of publication, copyright

> ***Example****: <u>War</u>, by Thomas Jackson, Chronicle Books, NY, 1999*

Internet Sources

Author (if provided), title of the page you are using on this site, title of overall website, date of article/last date site was updated, date you viewed the site, website address

> ***Example****: Giovanni Antonio, "Allies," "WWII in America,"*
>
> *June 2002, viewed November 8, 2010, www.ww2americans.com*

Periodical Sources

Author(s), title, volume, issue, year of publication, page numbers, medium of publication

> ***Example*** *Thomas Jackson, "Necessity of Nuclear Weapons," Military Quarterly,*
>
> *25.2, 1996, print*

See Appendix C for a reproducible source list.

Step Three of Frontward Mapping: Note Evidence

First you must know what evidence is:

1. It is something you did not know before you read it,

2. It is related to your general thesis and/or supports a specific claim.

Next, you must know how to document that evidence:

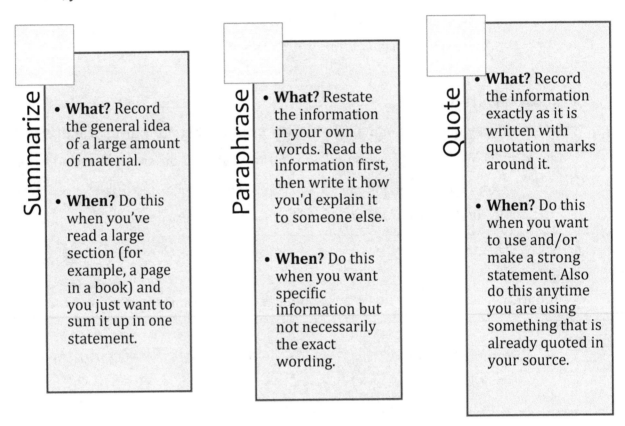

Summarize

- **What?** Record the general idea of a large amount of material.

- **When?** Do this when you've read a large section (for example, a page in a book) and you just want to sum it up in one statement.

Paraphrase

- **What?** Restate the information in your own words. Read the information first, then write it how you'd explain it to someone else.

- **When?** Do this when you want specific information but not necessarily the exact wording.

Quote

- **What?** Record the information exactly as it is written with quotation marks around it.

- **When?** Do this when you want to use and/or make a strong statement. Also do this anytime you are using something that is already quoted in your source.

There are many ways to take notes. By the time you have become an experienced researcher, you will have tried many ways to find the best fit for you. For now, however, you will use the note-card method. This will allow you to order the evidence you find in a way that best proves your position and tells the story of your research.

Follow the note-card method as directed on the following page, even if you don't see the point. If you TRUST THE PROCESS, the process will serve you. If you don't, you'll end up creating a lot more work for yourself in the long run.

Note-card process:

1. Once you deem a source reliable and useful, note its source information (see page 23) either on the provided source list (see appendix C) or separate paper. LABEL THE SOURCE with a letter (A, B, C, etc.).

2. All notes should be written on one side of a note card. Ideally these will be index cards (even half-index cards work fine), all of the same size.

3. PUT ONLY ONE PIECE OF INFORMATION ON EACH CARD. USE ONLY ONE SIDE OF EACH CARD. If your information goes on longer than one side of one card, you have too much. Even if it's a quote, break it in half using ellipsis (…) if you need to. It's best to keep your note to one phrase or sentence if possible.

4. Instead of writing the source's full publication information on this card, write the SOURCE LETTER. You must also note THE PAGE NUMBER for a book or periodical or the DATE VIEWED for an Internet source (see examples below).

A *sample note-card* for a <u>book</u> or periodical source looks like this:

"The tactics of the Japanese indicate they will never surrender." President Truman, July 1945.   Source C, page 52

A *sample note-card* for an <u>internet</u> source looks like this:

"The tactics of the Japanese indicate they will never surrender." President Truman, July 1945.   Source C, 3/25*

*This is the date you viewed the site

You may be tempted to number your cards as you do them; **don't**. There will be a process for that later. For now, secure them as you go with a rubber band, in an envelope, or index cardholder.

Need a Guideline?
Find out from your instructor how many pages are required for your paper. Then gather about 5-6 cards for each page required (5 page requirement = about 30 cards). This will be a great start from which to launch step four.

See Appendix D for reproducible note cards.

Step Four of Frontward Mapping: Develop Thesis

Remember we talked about this being a research paper and not a book report? A report is just a recounting of the facts; *a research paper uses facts written in a way that proves your thesis, or your position, on your topic.*

A thesis is not an announcement of your topic ("This paper will be about..."); it is your position on a topic. As such, your thesis should be strong, clear, concise, and without a doubt show the reader your position on the topic and the point you will prove with your research.

First, organize yourself and analyze what you have.

    a) Lay out your evidence cards so that you can see and read them all.

    b) Consider these questions:

> ➢ Toward what point does your research seem to lean?

> ➢ What questions are coming up for you as you research?

> ➢ Does your research seem to prove something? Is it showing you something is true, false, significant, or controversial?

    c) Consider your answers and develop an overall position about your topic. This will be your thesis.

Examples: Moving from Topic to Thesis

I have about 30 cards gathered on my topic and I see a few themes:

- America wants the war over
- Japan won't surrender
- The Allies gathered to discuss drastic options to force Japanese surrender

What positions could I take on this information?

On the following page are example theses based on my topic, dropping the Atom Bomb. For each thesis example, notes about positives and negatives are provided.

Thesis Examples

Below Average	Average	Above Average
• I think the U.S. was right to drop the bomb and you will too after reading my paper.	• The U.S. was right to drop the Atom Bomb on the Japanese in August of 1945.	• The United States was desperate to end WWII and since the Japanese had no intention of surrendering, the U.S. was totally justified in dropping the Atom Bomb.

Excellent
After four years and thousands of lives lost, by August 1945 the U.S. was desperate to end WWII. The government compiled strong evidence that showed the only way to bring the war with Japan to an end was to do something drastic and devastating; therefore, the U.S. was justified in dropping the Atom Bomb.

For each thesis example, notes about positives and negatives are as follows:

Below Average: I think the U.S. was right to drop the bomb and you will, too, after reading my paper.

- Is it grammatically accurate with correct spelling? Yes. That's the only thing keeping this thesis from the "poor" level.

- NEVER use "I think" in your thesis. It's clear you think that or you wouldn't be writing it. In addition, it invites the reader to say, "Well that's what you think, not what I think." Be strong and stand behind your thesis.

- NEVER use "you" anywhere in a research paper. You should be arguing a point, not talking to the reader. Stay focused and don't personalize it for the reader.

- There is no sense of context in this example. It might have happened yesterday in Nebraska.

Average: The U.S. was right to drop the Atom Bomb on the Japanese in August of 1945.

- The lack of "I think" and "you" automatically makes this better.

- Context is present, but not specific.
- It's concise and clear, but short on depth.

Above Average: The United States was desperate to end WWII and since the Japanese had no intention of surrendering, the U.S. was totally justified in dropping the Atom Bomb.

- With concise, clear, and strong language, this is a solid thesis.
- There are, however, two overarching generalizations here: "no intention" and "totally justified." You really don't know that, so change the language to that of research instead of judgment.

Excellent: After four years and thousands of lives lost, by August 1945 the U.S. was desperate to end WWII. The government compiled strong evidence that showed the only way to bring the war with Japan to an end was to do something drastic and devastating; therefore, the U.S. was justified in dropping the Atom Bomb.

- A two-sentence thesis is not always recommended/allowed in high school research papers. In college, sometimes a 3-5 sentence thesis is expected. Carefully review the guidelines provided by your instructor.
- Regardless of length requirement, note about our thesis that it provides context, sophistication, and a strong sense that you know what you are talking about. For longer theses, consider adding a counter-clause, specific examples of what evidence you're going to include, and/or a "So what?" statement. (More information about these additions is available in the thesis checklist in the appendix.)
- There is a strong tone of educated research in this thesis. There is no judgment, nor exclamation, just a calm sense of what was happening and what had to happen as a result.
- The reader is left with a strong sense of what you will prove and trusts you to get on with doing it.

See Appendix B for a thesis checklist.

Not Feeling Ready to Write your Thesis?

Sometimes starting with the thesis is overwhelming. You know the general areas you want to cover and even what you want to say about them, but you don't feel quite ready to establish a thesis.

Is this you? Consider moving on to the next section about claims first then, once your claims are done, you can come back here to build a thesis around those claims. This is very common, so feel free to test it out to see if it

Step Five of Frontward Mapping: Breakdown Claims

Claims come directly out of your thesis.

To develop your claims, first break down your excellent thesis; second, make claims out of your pieces in a way that they both take a position and, when added up, prove your thesis. Follow the model below for direction.

Here's our excellent thesis:

> After four years and thousands of lives lost, by August 1945 the U.S. was desperate to end WWII. The government compiled strong evidence that showed the only way to bring the war with Japan to an end was to do something drastic and devastating; therefore, the U.S. was justified in dropping the Atom Bomb.

Here's our excellent thesis broken down into parts:

> 1-After four years and thousands of lives lost, by August 1945 the U.S. was desperate to end WWII.
>
> 2-The government compiled strong evidence that showed the only way to bring the war with Japan to an end was to do something drastic and devastating;
>
> 3-therefore, the U.S. was justified in dropping the Atom Bomb.

How Do I Make Claims out of these Parts?

Claims are like subtopics because they break down the thesis down into more manageable parts; but they are different because *claims take a position.* You will prove each claim one at a time through your research and, together, they will add up to prove your thesis.

Claim Examples

The following are claims that strongly support the example thesis. For each notice:

- Average claims are clear and concise, take a position, and clearly define the coming paragraph(s).
- Above average claims do all of the above, plus provide a bit of context.
- Excellent claims do all of the above with sophisticated, researched-based tone and language. They also convey the same idea as part of the thesis with a bit more detail (and without using the same words).

Claim One Examples **based on, "After four years and thousands of lives lost, by August 1945 the U.S. was desperate to end WWII."**

- **Average**: The U.S. was desperate.
- **Above Average**: After four years of bloody battle, the U.S. was desperate to end WWII.
- **Excellent:** The human and monetary costs of the war were spiraling and Americans at home were anxious both financially and emotionally; the U.S. government was desperate to end WWII.

Claim Two Examples **based on, "The government compiled strong evidence that showed the only way to end war with Japan was to do something drastic and devastating..."**

- **Average**: The government had evidence that the Japanese were not ever going to give up.
- **Above Average**: The U.S. government had strong evidence that drastic measures were required to end WWII.
- **Excellent:** Even as it appeared inevitable that Japan would eventually lose the war, it was clear that a drastic and devastating move by the Allies was necessary to force the surrender of the Japanese.

Claim Three Examples **based on, "...therefore, the U.S. was justified in dropping the Atom Bomb."**

- **Average**: The U.S. was justified in dropping the Atom Bombs.

- **Above Average**: Although there were other options to end the war, the U.S. was justified in dropping the two Atom Bombs on Japan.

- **Excellent:** President Truman was presented with other options to force Japanese surrender, however none of them would be as devastating as the dropping of the Atom Bombs on Hiroshima and Nagasaki, Japan.

See Appendix B for a claims checklist.

Step Six of Frontward Mapping: Collect Further Evidence

At this point you have 5-6 cards of evidence per page required, a thesis, and a set of claims. Now is the time move forward to find more evidence.

Reminders:

1. Use high-quality sources. You may want to re-read page 22 to remind yourself what kind of sources are viable and which you should avoid.

2. If you are looking for something specific, narrow your search accordingly. You no longer want to search for "atom bomb," when you really want to know about what people thought about the bomb. In that case you'd search for something like, "different opinions of atom bomb testing in 1945."

3. If necessary, revisit pages 24-26 about rules for note cards. Now is not the time to get lazy. Write every source on your source page and note every piece of evidence properly. Doing so now will save you a lot of time and grief in the long run.

Need a Guideline?

Your goal for this step is to find 4-5 more cards per page requirement before moving on to step 7. (A 5-page requirement with 4-5 more cards per page means you must have an approximate total of 50 cards before continuing.)

A note to the very attentive:
You may have noticed the recommendation for number of cards and a few other minor details are different in the frontward mapping section as opposed to the backward mapping section. This is intentional; an extra layer is involved in working frontward, so the process is a bit different.

Step Seven of Frontward Mapping: Pause

You now need to be certain your thesis and claims are working with your evidence so you can have specific direction for your last bit of research.

"Pause" has three goals: **Organize** your information to see what you have so far; **Consider** the story you are trying to tell; **Proceed** with researching the evidence you still need to find.

Organize

1. Spread your cards out over a large surface so you can see and read all the evidence you have so far.

2. Make a pile of evidence for each of your claims. If you find your evidence isn't clearly represented by the claims you have, group them together logically and you can readjust your claims later by referencing back to pages 31-34. If you find a few of your cards don't quite fit, put them aside for now.

3. Within each claim pile, put the cards in an order that start to tell the story you aim to tell. You'll notice some gaps; that's the point of this whole activity. **This is a time to make what I call a "Remember!" sheet. This is where you'll keep track of all the things you want to remember as you proceed**. Make a note about your information gaps and move on.

4. Now that your claim piles are in order, decide which claim pile goes first, second, and so on.

Consider

1. Is your original thesis supported by your claims? If yes, proceed. If it's questionable, refer back to pages 27-30 to revise your thesis.
2. Are your original claims supported by the evidence you have found? If so, proceed. If it's questionable, refer to pages 31-34 to revise your claims.
3. After you've completed the two suggestions above, I'd strongly consider finding a friend or two to help you be sure you've considered all possibilities. Often times we know what we want to say and take for granted that we're saying it; reading your information aloud to someone else is the best way for you to check your self and your work.

Proceed

1. Spread out the cards for your first claim pile again.
2. Reread your first claim and then reread the evidence you already have.
3. What more do you need to prove this claim? Is there a supporting statistic, a quote, one more piece of information that would really prove your point to the reader? Go to your "Remember!" sheet and note what you need to find for claim one.
4. Restack your first claim pile and move on to the second claim pile. Repeat steps #1-3 for each of your claim piles.
5. Restack all claim piles into the one large stack. Add any loose cards to either the front or the back. Rubber band or clip your cards to keep them in this general order, but DO NOT number them.

Step Eight of Frontward Mapping: Collect Last Evidence

Now it's time to finish that research. Repeating the process from page 34, fill in the last of your research gaps by getting as much accurate, interesting evidence as possible to prove your claims and thesis.

Reminders:

1. Continue to use high-quality sources.

2. You likely only have a few very specific things left to find. Narrow your search significantly. (Remember the Atom Bomb example on page 34?)

3. If necessary, revisit pages 24-26 about rules for note-cards. Now is not the time to get lazy. Remember to write every source on your source page and note every piece of evidence properly. Doing so now will save you a lot of time and grief in the long run.

**When you are done with this process,
proceed to the next section on final outlines,
drafts, and citations.**

Final Steps

Before getting started with these final steps, consider whether you need further help with the writing process. Many students struggle not only with the research part of a paper, but also the writing. If you think that may be you as well, consider picking up a book called *Easy Writer*, by Andrea Lunsford. In that book there are more in depth explanations of how to complete the final steps I've listed below.

First: Organize and Outline

This is the place to be sure your evidence is complete and, in fact, proves your claims and thesis. You will throw some research out that you find doesn't work and may have to re-order what is left in a way that best tells the story.

> Many students want to skip outlining. Understandably, you are tired and want to just get this thing done, but resist the urge to jump ahead. This step is <u>critical</u> to an easy drafting of what will be the final paper.

Organize

1. Spread your cards out over a large surface so you can see and read all the evidence you have so far.

2. Organize your cards into claim piles. Your claims should be solid by now; if not, you will have time to revise them when you outline.

3. As you sort, you may come across cards that don't fit into claims and/or cards you want to use elsewhere (like the introduction or conclusion). Pull those out for now.

4. Within each claim pile, put your cards in logical, storytelling order. Establish the order by how best it flows together to prove your point.

5. Now that each of your claim piles are in order, decide which claim pile goes first, second, and so on.

6. If you pulled out cards for the introduction, put them on top in the order you want to use them. If you pulled out cards for the conclusion, put them on the bottom in the order you want them to go. If you have cards that don't fit, recycle them. When you are done you will have one stack of cards that tells the story of your entire paper.

7. NOW, NUMBER THEM! Write a number on the top right corner of each card, chronologically from number one. (If you have twenty-five cards, they should be numbered 1-25.) These numbers are critically important for the outlining, the drafting, and the citation process.

Outline:

What and Why

-This is the skeleton of your first draft. A solid outline means an easy draft.

-Remember the purpose of the introduction is to introduce the topic to your reader. Go back to your background search for the basic who, what, when, why, of your topic and list those facts in the order that one, helps the reader understand and, two, peaks their interest in wanting to read more.

-If you have followed all of the steps as instructed so far, this won't take you as much time as you fear because you don't have to write in your evidence, just the number of the note card.

Until now there has been a formula for all the steps. Here, you are freer to do what works for you, within a few parameters.

Options and Things to Notice about Final Outline Example:

1. You may do a visual, web-like outline or a linear one like the example on the following pages.

2. You may want to use a note card in your introduction or you may not.

3. I write out the full text of the thesis and the claims in the outline because it keeps my head clear about what I'm doing and the flow of the paper. If you don't want to, you can just write "thesis" and then write out the full text of the thesis when you go to do your draft.

4. For the evidence, I simply note the card number and wait for the draft to type what the card says.

5. In the sample outline, you'll see the word **commentary**.* That is where, if this were my real outline, I would write down my thoughts and/or explanations. For your outline, you should note what you are going to write. There is no need for complete sentences, just jot down your points of commentary and move on.

6. Some cards will go together, others will require you to add your commentary between cards. You will have to figure that out as you outline. *As a rule, use no more than three cards before you add your own words.* Add your own thoughts and/or explanation as much as possible to show what you understand about what the evidence says.

7. Some claims will require one paragraph while others will need multiple paragraphs. Look for natural breaks in your evidence.

---

*Commentary is challenging for most students. Please see Appendix B for "Commentary Basics" and a commentary checklist.

Final Outline Example

I.   Introduction
- a. WWII global war lasting roughly five years
- b. Allies and Axis powers
- c. Hundreds of thousands of lives lost, impact on millions by 1945
- d. Potsdam conference abroad, Manhattan Project at home
- e. Card #1
- f. (Thesis) After four years and thousands of lives, by August 1945 the U.S. was desperate to end WWII. The government compiled strong evidence that showed the only way to bring the war with Japan to an end was to do something drastic and devastating; therefore, the U.S. was justified in dropping the Atom Bomb.

II.   (Claim One) The human and monetary costs of the war were spiraling and Americans at home were anxious both financially and emotionally; the U.S. government was desperate to end WWII.
- a. #2
- b. #3
- c. Commentary
- d. #4
- e. Commentary
- f. #5
- g. #6
- h. Commentary

III.   Card #7
- a. Commentary
- b. #8
- c. #9
- d. Commentary

Remember:

- This is a SAMPLE outline. I don't know what number cards go together for you, where you should stop for commentary, or where your paragraph breaks will be. That's something you'll have to work out.

- I wrote the word "commentary" because this is a SAMPLE; you need to actually jot down ideas for what you will discuss/explain when you go to write your draft.

IV.   (Claim Two) Even as it appeared inevitable that Japan would eventually lose the war, it was clear that a drastic and devastating move by the Allies was necessary to force the surrender of the Japanese.

(The outline continues in this manner until completion.)

As you are writing the outline, you might find a few more cards don't fit. If so, recycle them and RENUMBER YOUR REMAINING CARDS. The cards <u>must</u> go in a chronological order both for citation purposes (if you are using footnotes) as well as your own ability to stay organized.

Second: First Draft and Citations within the Document

First, set up your basic formatting. Most instructors require double-spaced type with one-inch margins, page numbers, and a 12-point readable font. Check with your instructor for alternative and/or additional requirements.

With your completed outline beside you, type your rough draft. This is not time for perfection; this is the time for you to get all your work in one document from start to finish. Your rough draft should be complete, from the introduction to the conclusion, with the thesis, and every claim and piece of evidence typed in.

Before you start, however, you need to familiarize yourself with citations. These are the notes within the document that show which pieces of evidence are from sources other than you. This is a critical step that cannot be overlooked, no matter how much you wish you could.

As you move through your draft, thank yourself for following the directions during the evidence collection phase.

Citations within Your Draft
Without citations you put yourself in danger of being accused of plagiarism, which brings a zero on your assignment and disciplinary action from your school. *Different disciplines have different requirements for citations. Please check with your instructor before completing this task.*

Option One: MLA Style
This is the usual choice for research in the area of humanities, although that is not always the case. To use MLA-style citations within the document, follow these basic guidelines:

- After the piece of evidence (these are your note cards, remember) put the last name of the author and the page number where you found the information with no comma in between and the ending punctuation after the citation.
  - President Truman said "The tactics of the Japanese indicate(d) they (would) never surrender." (Abbot 120).

- You also can cite the author within your sentence and then note the page number where you found the information afterward.
  - Jane Abbot quoted President Truman as saying, "The tactics of the Japanese indicate(d) they (would) never surrender (120).

For more information, including how to cite different kinds of sources (websites, etc.), go to the following website for a commonly used MLA Guide:

http://owl.english.purdue.edu/owl/resource/747/01/

Option Two: APA Style

This is the usual choice for research in the area of science and social science, although that is not always the case. To use APA-style citations within the document, follow these basic guidelines:

- APA standards include using the author, the year of publication, and the page number of the source. It can be done in a number of ways, but usually includes some kind of reference to the author within the sentence itself.
  - According to Abbot (2010) President Truman said, "The tactics of the Japanese indicate(d) they (would) never surrender." (p. 120).

  - She quoted President Truman as saying, "The tactics of the Japanese indicate(d) they (would) never surrender (Abbot, 2010, p.120).

For more information, including how to cite different kinds of sources (websites, etc.), go to the following website for a commonly used APA Guide:

http://owl.english.purdue.edu/owl/resource/560/01/

Option Three: CM Style (CMS)

This is the usual choice for research in the area of English, although that is not always the case. CMS citations generally require footnotes as opposed to in-text citation. If your instructor asks you to do something differently but does not give you specific information about how to do it, check this website for a commonly used CMS Guide:

http://owl.english.purdue.edu/owl/resource/717/01/

If that does not give you enough information and/or the information you need, go online for a 30-day trial to the Chicago Manual of Style Online, which you can find at this website: **http://www.chicagomanualofstyle.org/16/contents.html**

Some Specific Directions on Footnotes

Every computer is different, however the directions below will work with most word processing programs. Use your outline to type your draft. When you get to the spot that says #1 for your first note card, type out the contents written on the card, then cite the source for that piece of evidence by following the directions below.

a) Type in the information from your note card. With the cursor **after** the punctuation, go to the toolbar at the top and click "insert."

b) Scroll down for the word "footnote." (If your computer doesn't have it, it may have "reference;" click that, then click "footnote.")

c) A menu will come up asking you how you want to footnote. Choose chronological/automatic (1, 2, 3...) and have the footnotes show up at the bottom of each page. Once those settings are in place, click "ok."

d) Your first footnote should show up at the bottom of the page.[1]

---

[1] The computer program will automatically send you here. See letter e on the next page for directions about what to do down here.

e) Now that you're down there, cite your source. Whatever source is noted on your card, refer to your source list for its corresponding publishing information.

  i.   Different sources require different kinds of citations. Look below for an example of how a citation for a book may look.[2]

  ii. In addition, once you've cited the source once, you do it differently the next time. Look below for an example.[3]

  iii. Please check the suggested CMS source guides listed to be sure you are citing the information in the correct way. For a quick look at how to cite sources for footnotes at the bottom of the page, see this website: **http://www.oberlin.edu/faculty/svolk/citation.htm**

f) After EACH and EVERY card, you must insert a footnote. It doesn't matter if the card came from the same source or not; it doesn't matter if it is a continuation in thought from the card before. EACH AND EVERY TIME you type information from a card, insert a footnote.

Whichever in-text citation method you use, continue it throughout the typing of your draft.

---

[2] Mario the Dog, *My sense of WW2.* (New York: University Press, 2005), 100-101.
[3] Abbott p. 210

Third: Edits

The editing process should include at least two self-edits and one or two peer edits. Each will bring to your paper a different perspective; as such, your paper will end up better developed, both in content and in structure. Appendix E has sample edit guidelines.

Self-Edit

You should complete the first edit of your paper. Give your paper a read-through so you do not waste someone else's time with obvious typos and spelling mistakes. If you need more specific guidance than what is provided here, see Appendix E.

Read your thesis and claims again and consider checking them against the checklist in Appendix B as well. They should be arguable, sophisticated, and clear. Are they? Then Read your paper from start to finish again, aloud this time. As you read, note your thoughts on the following:

1. Look carefully for places where you could add more of your own commentary.
2. Consider the flow of the paper: does it read easily or is it choppy? Is it in logical order or should something be moved around? (NOTE! If you move evidence, you must also change your citations. Do so carefully.)
3. Does the introduction really introduce your paper and the conclusion really concludes it?
4. Do the thesis and claims meet expectations or should they be reworded a bit to make them stronger?

Only when you have done a through read-through and edit of your own paper should you feel comfortable passing it on for someone else's opinion. Other people shouldn't have to interpret your work's value simply because you haven't done the work to show them your best effort; you should always make every effort to do your best you do so they can see it for exactly what it is, not what it could be.

Based on the Self Edit(s), make necessary revisions before continuing to Peer Edits.

Peer Edits

If you want someone to check your spelling and grammar, handing it to a trusted person may be enough. If, however, you want a full edit on all aspects of your paper, you need to give her/him more specific direction.

Your instructor may have a specific form for a peer to use as s/he edits your paper. If not, consider using one of the forms provided in Appendix E. Be sure to also tell your editor about any other information your instructor requires.

A note on peer edits: you don't have to accept suggestions. It is neither your peers' paper nor your peers' grade. It's yours. If you don't feel good about a suggested change, don't make it. However do consider their suggestions thoughtfully and make all changes that feel right to you.

Based on the Peer Edit(s), make the necessary revisions before moving on to Final Draft Preparation.

See Appendix E for reproducible edit forms.

Fourth: Final Draft Preparation

Once your paper has been thoughtfully edited a minimum of three times, *with revisions made at each stage*, you can safely assume you have a solid paper and are almost done.

The following three things must be done before you can turn in your work.

1. Follow all Final Draft Preparation Guides

Just as you had to use the appropriate in-text citation style called for by your instructor, so too must you follow rules for the title and reference pages. On the following pages are directions, samples, and links for more information on how to complete them.

2. Putting it all Together

You have worked so hard on this project, shouldn't it look like it? First impressions count and a research project is no exception. Be mindful of keeping your paper as polished and professional looking as possible.

3. Congratulations are in Order

Don't skip this step. Many students will have quit before completion; others will have cut corners and compromised a successful paper. You didn't. You stuck to your commitment and followed through. Take pride in your work and in yourself.

From me to you, Congratulations!

Reference Page

A reference page is included so your reader can see where you got your information in order to check how accurately you represented those sources and/or to do more of their own research related to something you wrote.

Use your source page to complete the reference page for your final draft. Start by numbering your sources alphabetically by author's last name. If no author is listed, use the title of the source. *This must be done first.*

Once your list is alphabetized, type your reference page according to the style required by your instructor. All reference lists start on a separate page placed at the end of the paper with the sources listed alphabetically by the author's last name, if available (otherwise you may alphabetize by the title of the work). The three styles require basically the same information from each kind of source, differing mostly in formatting and order of information.

Below are examples for book and webpage example sources only. They include both the information required and the order and formatting of that information. Website addresses are noted for more information and/or how to cite other types of sources.

MLA Style

Works Cited

Last Name, First Name of author. *Title.* Place of Publication: Name of
      Publisher, Year of Publication. Type of Publication.

Last Name, First Name of Author/Editor "Article Title," *Title of Website.* <u>URL</u>
      <u>address</u>, Date Viewed.

For more information on MLA Works Cited pages, visit this commonly referenced website: **http://owl.english.purdue.edu/owl/resource/747/05/**

APA Style

> ### References
>
> Last Name, First Name of the author. (Year of Publication). _Title_. Place of Publication:
> > Publisher.
>
> Last Name, First Name of Author/Editor. (Date of Publication). "Article Title."
> > _Title of Website_. Retrieved from URL address.

For more information on APA Reference pages, visit this commonly referenced website:

http://owl.english.purdue.edu/owl/resource/560/05/

CM Style (CMS)

> ### Bibliography
>
> Last Name, First Name of author. _Title_. Place of Publication: Name of
> > Publisher, Year of Publication.
>
> Last Name, First Name of Author/Editor "Title of the Article." _Title of Website_.
> > Publication date/access date. URL Address.

For more information on CMS Bibliography pages, visit this commonly referenced

website: **http://owl.english.purdue.edu/owl/resource/717/05/**

Title Page and Page Numbers

Give your paper a title--NOT, "My Research Paper" or "A Paper on the Atom Bomb." Consider your thesis and how that can become an intriguing title.

MLA Style

Most users of MLA say that a title page is unnecessary. Instead your name, instructor's name, course name, and due date should be on the top left of the first page. Give each its own line and double space between lines. On the next line, center the title. Then, on the next line, indent your paragraph and begin.

MLA style requires your last name and the page number at the top of the page, justified to the right. To do so, insert a header that includes that information.

For a sample MLA first page visit this website:

http://owl.english.purdue.edu/owl/resource/747/1/

Last Name   1

Your Name

Your Instructor's Name

Your Course Name

Due Date

                                                Title

    Begin writing your paper's introduction right here.

APA Style

APA style requires the following information on your title page: Running Head, Page Number, Title, Name, and School. Insert a header. Include the phrase, "Running Head," your title in capital letters, and the page number. If you did it correctly, it will run on every page of your document.

Then, click somewhere else on this page (which will close the header), center your curser and return down several spaces to type your title. On the next line, type your name. Under that, type your school's name. These three parts of the title page should be double-spaced and centered at the top-middle half of the page.

For a sample APA title page visit this website:

http://owl.english.purdue.edu/owl/resource/560/01/

Running head: TITLE OF PAPER   1

                                    Title of Paper

                                    Your Name

                                    Your School

CM Style (CMS)

This style requires the following information on your title page: title, name, course name, and due date. The title should be in all capital letters in the center of the page in the top half. Your name, course name, and date should be single-spaced, each on its own line, toward the bottom half in the center of the page.

Page numbers should be in a header starting on the first page of text (not your title page). Insert a header on this page, then insert page numbers, and be sure to format those numbers to begin on the proper page.

For a sample CMS title page visit this website:

http://owl.english.purdue.edu/owl/resource/717/02/

TITLE OF PAPER

Your Name
Your Class Title
Due Date

Appendix

The proceeding pages are available for reproduction. Should you want access to an electronic version, which you can manipulate in order to customize it for your purposes, email info@dirtpathpublishing.com.

Appendix A: Background Check

<u>**Background Check**</u>
For your topic, gather the information below. Use your book, the Internet, an encyclopedia, or friends, remembering the point of this is to get a general idea about your topic before pushing forward with specific research.

If you discover that while working on this background you can't find information or it seems boring, CHANGE YOUR TOPIC WHILE YOU CAN!

SOURCES USED FOR BACKGROUND:

Developing a Topic
I think my research will be on _____

1. Four Ws and the H
    • What is your topic about? (Give a general overview)

    • Who was involved?

    • When did it take place?

    • Where did it take place?

    • How did the topic start and finish? (Or is it still around and why?)

2. Context (What was happening in America during this time period? What was the general feeling of society in general and/or in regard to your topic?)

3. Perspective (How might different groups of people - race, gender, social/economic class, age - view this topic?)

4. Impact on History (How did this event influence America then and today?)

5. On a scale of 1-10, how interested are you in this topic? Explain.

Appendix B: Checklists

Thesis Checklist

Check your thesis against the following list. If adjustments need to be made, do so before moving on. If you feel confused, reread the examples and apply the advice to your own thesis.

1. The thesis takes a position about a topic, rather than simply announcing what the topic of the paper will be.

2. Thesis is absent of "I think," "I," and "you"

3. Thesis provides accurate and meaningful context.

4. Thesis uses research based tone and language, avoiding all generalizations and judgments.

5. Thesis provides a clear and strong sense of what the forthcoming evidence will prove.

For longer thesis (3-5 sentence) requirements, consider adding the following:

- A Counter-Clause: this is a statement that acknowledges the other opinions about the topic. For our thesis example this might include something like, "Some say the Atom Bomb was a gross overuse of power that needlessly injured hundreds of thousands of people..."

- Specific Examples: Some instructors like to know ahead of time what evidence you will be including. For our example this might include something like, "War strategists agree that..."

- So-What: this is a statement that addresses why readers should care about your topic and your particular position. For our example this might include something like, "War is a horrific time for all involved and sometimes a nation must decide to end it in equally horrific ways…"

Claims Checklist

Check each claim against the following list. If adjustments need to be made, do so before moving on. If you feel confused, reread the examples and apply the advice to your own claims.

1. The claim is clear and concise.

2. The claim takes a position.

3. The claim clearly defines what will be in the coming paragraph(s) and gives the reader accurate and meaningful context.

4. The claim uses research-based tone and language, avoiding all generalizations and judgments.

Evidence Checklist

Check your evidence against the following list. If adjustments need to be made, do so before moving on. If you feel confused, reread the examples and apply the advice to your own evidence.

1. The evidence is comes from a reliable source.
2. The evidence is accurate.
3. The evidence is appropriate to my topic/claim/thesis.
4. If the evidence is a quote or written word for word as the source's author wrote, quotations are used.
5. I know the exact source of the evidence.

Commentary Basics

This is usually the most difficult step for students for three reasons: one, they don't feel like they know what to say; two, they are unsure that what they do have to say is "right;" and, three, they live lives that are so rushed they rarely practice the skill of slowing down to take the time to really explain their thoughts. *Patience and confidence* are the characteristics you need to develop on in order to be successful with commentary.

Commentary should:

-Be two sentences or more in length. Write the first sentence, then think, "So what? What is this supposed to tell people?" Then, write about that.

-Be relevant to the evidence and claim. After you write it, double check. It needs to clearly connect. Don't announce that it connects ("This shows connection because...") Just show us.

-Provide connections. Don't force your reader to try to read your mind; connect the dots for them by clearly showing why you chose what you did and what point you are trying to prove.

-Avoid phrases like, "I chose this because..." We know you chose it, it's right there! Don't introduce the commentary; just write what would have been the next part of the sentence which, in fact, is the commentary.

Idea for the More Auditory Learner

Triads: Sit with two other students. One talks, one listens, one observes. The talker should tell the listener what the claim is, what the evidence is, and how the two connect. The listener's job is to probe with questions (tell me why, what makes you say that, how does this work"). The observer should be noting the talker's answers. This should continue for the duration of the evidence for this claim. When the claim is finished, students may continue with other claims or switch roles and repeat. After everyone has had a chance to talk through their claims, each should have a list of commentary to flesh out and add to their papers. Go through your list and highlight the parts of the commentary you think best meet the checklist requirements.

Idea for the More Visual Learner

<u>Mapping</u>: Write your claim in the middle of the paper. Write your evidence around it (shortened versions will do). Off each piece of evidence, note your thoughts about it. What does each piece of evidence mean? How does it connect to the claim?
What should the reader understand about why you chose this evidence? Each piece of evidence should have a lot notes around it. When you are done, go back with a highlighter and mark the parts of the commentary you think best meet the commentary requirements.

Commentary Checklist

Check your commentary against the following list, during both the outline and draft phase.

1. The commentary is two or more sentences in length each time.
2. The commentary is relevant to the evidence and claim.
3. The commentary provides connections that show why I chose what I did and what point I'm trying to make
4. The commentary does not rely on opening phrases like, "I chose this because…" or, "This shows…" Instead, it just gives thoughtful explanations and insightful connections without first introducing them as such.

Appendix C: Source List

Remember:
-   **Book Sources**
    Title, author, publisher, city of publication, copyright.

-   **Internet Sources**
    Author (if provided), title of the page you are using on this site, title of overall website, date of article/last date site was updated, date you viewed the site, website address.

Source A:

Source B:

Source C:

Source D:

Source E:

Source F:

Appendix D: Note cards

Fact:	Fact:
Source: Page #/Date Viewed	Source: Page #/Date Viewed
Fact:	Fact:
Source: Page #/Date Viewed	Source: Page #/Date Viewed
Fact:	Fact:
Source: Page #/Date Viewed	Source: Page #/Date Viewed
Fact:	Fact:
Source: Page #/Date Viewed	Source: Page #/Date Viewed
Fact:	Fact:
Source: Page #/Date Viewed	Source: Page #/Date Viewed

Appendix E: Edits
Self–Edit

Name of Writer _____

1. Read your paper **aloud** to yourself or, if you'd rather, to a partner
    *   Listen to your voice.
    *   Make any spelling/grammar corrections on the paper as you go. Watch for those commonly missed mistakes that not even the computer picks up during spell check (advise/advice, it's/its, from/form).

2. What did you learn from reading your paper aloud?

3. Does your paper have a logical flow form beginning to end and does it make sense?

4. In what ways is your paper interesting? What might you add to make it more interesting?

5. Where is your paper strongest?

6. Where does your paper need improvement?

7. How will you go about improving your paper?

8. What research are you still missing?

9. What questions do you have for the teacher about this research paper (either in content or in structure)?

Peer Edit Option

Things You Like

Clear   Insightful   Catchy   Powerful   Impressive
Strong Word Choice   Interesting   Strong Use of Evidence
(Notice: Good, Nice Job, Perfect, are not on this list. Be specific and supportive.)

Things that Need Work

Unclear   Develop   Needs More   Spelling?
Not Necessary   Awkward   Connection?   Confusing
(Notice: Learn to Spell, This is Terrible are not on this list. Be specific and constructive.)

All of the following sections must be addressed directly on the paper.
*Repeat steps 2-4 in bold below for each claim

1. Introduction
   a. Background facts and explanation
   b. Thesis (clarity, strength of position, arguable)

2. **Claims (Do the following for each claim)***
   a. Clarity
   b. Connection to thesis
   c. Wording

3. **Evidence***
   a. Enough to prove claim
   b. Quality and accuracy of evidence proves claim

4. **Explanation/Commentary***
   a. Writer clearly understands the evidence
   b. Writer helps reader understand how the evidence relates to the claim/thesis

5. Conclusion
   a. Summarizes main ideas
   b. Reminds reader of thesis
   c. Shows relevance and historical impact

6. In-Text Citations
   a. Notations are consistently made according to the directions

7. Reference Page
   a. Requirements are met in content and format

At the end of the paper, summarize in general terms what was strong and what needs to be improved before turning in the paper.

Peer Edit Option

Name of Writer:
Name of Editor:

Please do the following for all of the requirements below:
1. Label each requirement
    -- "Glow" if it's outstanding and after thinking long and hard
    there isn't anything you'd do to change it
    -- "Grow" if it needs some kind of work

2. For each "grow" please comment directly on the paper with your thoughts about how it could be improved.

3. Also, note any spelling/grammar issues directly on the paper.

Part of Paper	What is Required	Glow/Grow
Introduction	• Historical context • Background facts • Clear and arguable thesis	
Claim 1	• Clear and Arguable Claim • Enough context that evidence is understandable • Evidence is clear, proves claim, and plentiful • Commentary thoroughly explains evidence and ties to claim	
Claim 2	• Clear and Arguable Claim • Enough context that evidence is understandable • Evidence is clear, proves claim, and plentiful • Commentary thoroughly explains evidence and ties to claim	

Part of Paper	What is Required	Glow/Grow
Claim 3 (if present)	• Clear and Arguable Claim • Enough context that evidence is understandable • Evidence is clear, proves claim, and plentiful • Commentary thoroughly explains evidence and ties to claim	
Claim 4 (if present)	• Clear and Arguable Claim • Enough context that evidence is understandable • Evidence is clear, proves claim, and plentiful • Commentary thoroughly explains evidence and ties to claim	
Conclusion	• Summary of major ideas • Reminder of thesis • Shows relevance of topic and historical impact	
In-Text Citations	• Citations within document are made after every note card • Citations are complete as required by this discipline	
Reference Page	• All information required by this discipline is present • All sources are alphabetized	

Final Thoughts:

Acknowledgements

I write this series of books with a debt of gratitude to the teachers who came before me. My schoolteachers laid a foundation for me to do the work I do and my personal and professional mentors give me the strength and courage to continue that work each and every day. Too many to name, too many to count, I am blessed beyond measure.

To the 2,000 students who've passed through my door: you have taught me more about what it means to be good teacher and human being than any book ever could. Your stories move me; your resiliency inspires me; your presence made me better in all ways. Thank you for trusting me to be a part of your journey.

Specific thanks to Pam and Tovi for always being my first readers and invaluable sounding boards, to Carmen Klube, Amy Johnson Garcia and Mary Smathers for their keen-eyed editing skills, and to my students Devonte, Jazmin, and Alexis, for being my teachers this time around.

Thank you to Craig and Carmen for sharing their artistic talent and relentless assistance with the creation of the cover for this book. To Ryan Levesque of *Ebookit*, thank you for converting this book to an e-book format with grace and compassion for the questions I'm sure you thought would never end. To Dean Purvis of *Creative Tinder*, thank you for your ceaseless patience and good humor as we built my websites together.

To my mom, who made me go to summer school the year I got C's on my report card, thank you for pushing me to never settle for less than what was possible. The confidence you instilled in me has me believing there's nothing I can't do.

To my dad, Saint Mary's College, and the state of California, thank you for financing my higher education. It's a gift that keeps on giving, to me and those around me, each and every day.

To my children, who never fail to remind me what and who is really important, God has blessed me with innumerable gifts, but none can ever compare to the two of you.

And to my husband, Craig, a lifetime of thanks for your support. The spouses and partners of teachers are the unsung heroes of our vocation and you are no exception.